Peggy!
An awesome, great,
faithful servant of God.
Be blessed. Love Mom Porter
March 07- 2013

EFFECTIVE PRAYER WITHOUT CEASING

MAY I
PRAY WITH YOU ?

PRAYER COACH

MRS. CARRIE L. PORTER

May I Pray With You?
Effective Prayer Without Ceasing
By Mrs. Carrie L. Porter,
Prayer Coach

Contributing Writers:
Merle Ray, Katherine Claudette Campbell, and Pamela Christmas

Consultant, Merle Ray - www.MerleRay.com

Photographs by: LeeAndrea Benton
http://www.bentondesignphotography.com/

Published by Jubilee International Ministries
Printed in the U.S.A.
http://www.jubileepitt.com/

ISBN: 978-0-9852285-3-8

Unless otherwise indicated, Bible quotations are taken from the
American Standard Version (ASV)
Copyright © 1901 Public Domain.

MAY I PRAY WITH YOU?
Effective Prayer Without Ceasing

MAY I PRAY WITH YOU?
EFFECTIVE PRAYER WITHOUT CEASING
By Mrs. Carrie L. Porter,
Prayer Coach

TABLE OF CONTENTS

CHAPTER 6
PRAYER TIPS 101

CHAPTER 7
TYPES OF PRAYERS 108

FOREWORDS

In life, many people come along – some for a moment – others for a season – and some for a lifetime. Well, for Mom Carrie Porter and me, it has been a lifetime. She has been in my life for over 20 years. She and I have travelled together and enjoyed many meetings and lunches together where her line was always, *"May I pray with you?"* Even if you were hungry and ready to eat, she was going to pray with everyone that would let her.

As my life progressed, I was determined for her to see some of her dreams come true. One day, I said, *"Mom, I have finished my books; now it's your time to write yours."* She said, *"I have heard that before."* But I said, *"Since I have gone through the process, I can help you finish and achieve one of your goals and dreams."* I then called my publisher, Merle Ray, and as you can see, the rest is history. It is accomplished – and now Mom says, *"Hallelujah! I have two more to write!"* She is on a roll! I am so proud of my mom writing a book in her 80's! God certainly makes our dreams come true.

Read this book and discover the secret of moving God's heart. He will make your dreams come true!

Pastor Connie Brooks

Ministry is, and has been, the center of my life. I have ministered in Africa, from Uganda to Senegal and South Africa; as well as Saudi Arabia and India. Service, which is *ministry*, also placed me in secular settings such as political organizations, lobbying, nonprofits, and academia. Whether religious or secular, preaching or governance, I have not found a servant leader that surpasses Mrs. Carrie Porter. *Ma Porter* is the exemplar of living the adventurous, relevant life. And she does it as a life of prayer.

This book *"May I Pray With You?"* teaches basic, effective, fervent prayer. It also illustrates how to put *legs to your prayers* as a simple, powerful, results-producing evangelistic tool. Ma Porter draws on her years of experience and proven techniques in

Christian literature to teach us prayer. Using readable anecdotal style, it provides powerful truths and principles applicable to daily life centered on knowing God. Stirring you emotionally, challenging you cognitively, and inspiring you spiritually, it draws on Ma Porter's remarkable walk to show God's providence in our everyday associations.

The lady with the child at the Laundromat becomes more to you than just one of thousands. The concierge at the hotel you frequent is more than the consummate professional who remembers your favorite restaurant. The elderly person on the porch or out for a walk, whom you greet regularly, morphs into more than a cute old person. The employee becomes more than just *staff.* You become more than your role or title. This book brings alive with simple, yet striking illustrations the opportunities in our path to serve. It calls us to action in a personal, not violating way. From Ma Porter's encounters with luggage handlers and police officers, legislators and judges, lay ministers and senior pastors who serve thousands, we are provided a prayer portal to seize providence in vibrant, invigorating ways.

Moving from Lansing, Michigan to Pittsburgh was a great, new adventure for my family. Over 40 years I lived within five miles of my childhood home.

The lady who taught me to *type* on a manual typewriter also taught my older children to *keyboard* on a computer. Moving to the big city was a big deal. It felt like we had left everyone.

Then came Ma Porter. We had seen her for years during annual church meetings, but were barely acquainted. Upon arriving in Pittsburgh her warm embrace and patented *"May I pray with you?"* won us over. In a world of fast movement and *distant* close relationships, she was touchable, available, and took the initiative to care for us. Mothering or pastoring, leadership or coaching, whatever: she exhorted, admonished, and continually, frequently expressed love, commitment, and belief in me and my family. I shudder to think of making this family relocation without her.

Read this book and you will be reminded and convinced that: You matter! You can make a difference (if you don't care who gets the credit!) You can have an endless sense of value and self-acceptance! And you can have a prayer life that unveils that God has not forgotten you, knows your name, and each morning busies Himself with your every step!

MAY I PRAY WITH YOU?
Effective Prayer Without Ceasing

Be richly blessed and transformed by testimonies to your potential and destiny found in this book.

Reverend David A. Bell, Ph.D.

May I Pray with You? is a handbook on prayer. It is a guide that examines what prayer is, how to be victorious in prayer, and how to develop and maintain an effective fervent prayer life. Replete with scriptures, with profound simplicity, this book will not only teach you how to pray, but will help you gain greater insight into how God works through prayer, the role of the Holy Spirit in prayer, and how God uses prayer to accomplish His will in your life. This book is for anyone who desires to prevail in the kind of prayer that invokes the presence of the Holy Spirit, captures the heart of God, and makes manifest the promises of God in your life.

Reverend Mary Perdue, Ph.D.

DEDICATION

Writing this book is a rewarding journey. I am grateful to God, my Lord & Savior Jesus Christ, and to Pastor Connie Brooks, my spiritual daughter, who encouraged me and made it possible to write this legacy on prayer.

To the memory of my deceased husband; Lloyd Lawrence Porter, who loved God and His Word. Lloyd was committed to searching scriptures and praying daily. He loved, supported, and encouraged me continually to pray and praise God.

To the memory of my deceased daughter, Elsia Lucious Franklin, who was a Bible teacher, an intercessor, psalmist, worship leader, and a Christian counselor. Elsia loved God and her family and she led many souls to Jesus.

To my son, William Andrew Lucious, a faithful and supportive son. To my daughters, Katherine Lucious Jones, also known as, Katherine Claudette Campbell, and Pamela Lucious Christmas, two faithful and supportive daughters.

MAY I PRAY WITH YOU?
Effective Prayer Without Ceasing

INTRODUCTION

MAY I PRAY WITH YOU?

One morning in prayer God had me read Isaiah 60:1-5. After reading that scripture which spoke concerning *the glory of the Lord rising upon you,* in my spirit I heard the Lord say, *"I desire from you fervent, effectual intercessory prayer."* I said, *"Oh, yes, yes, Lord,"* because I thought that was what I was doing. After He repeated, *"fervent, effectual intercessory prayer,"* three times, I asked, *"Oh God, what is fervent, effectual intercessory prayer?"* I was weeping and repenting; then I listened.

The Lord said, *"fervent, effectual intercessory prayer, is praying what I want, and not what you think I want! The way to find out what I want is by asking Me and looking in My Word."* I said, "Thank you, Jesus." Now by following His instructions, I am enjoying being a faithful prayer warrior for our King.

Many years ago, He commissioned me to pray at the time of His visitation. He commanded me to pray for everyone that I would meet. I knew I was unable to accomplish that task in and of myself, so He gave me a strategy. The Lord said, *"I will bring faces, names, cities, states, and even countries before your eyes. Pray! Pray! Pray! I will also prompt you who to go to and ask, 'May I Pray With You?'"* It is now my daily delight to obey this awesome command. Hallelujah!

The goal of this book is to assist you in your efforts to have a productive effective prayer life. The examples presented reflect only a few of the experiences that God has done, is doing and will do in my life. None of us are perfect, but we all have the opportunity to call on the Name of the Lord, for repentance, salvation, guidance, direction, obedience, thanksgiving, praise and worship. *"I love them that love Me; and those that seek Me diligently shall find Me"* (Proverbs 8:17).

During my 80+ years of life, I've been impacted by countless members of the Body of Christ. God knows it is not my intent to omit anyone or take credit for anyone's work in presenting this book. Any omission of credit is only by mistake. For any such errors, I ask in advance for your forgiveness and support as I endeavor only to represent our Father's love and excellence.

MAY I PRAY WITH YOU?
Effective Prayer Without Ceasing

CHAPTER 1

A PRAYER OF BLESSING

Father, in the name of Jesus, I pray for every individual that reads this book. I pray for those persons who will come to know You as a result of this book. I pray for those who already know You; for those desiring a "layman's" understanding of how to come to You in prayer, and for those who have forgotten Your faithfulness to them.

"Father, help us to devote ourselves to prayer, obedience to God's Word, respecting and encouraging others daily."

I pray that we will be blessed abundantly. Father, bless our faithfulness to Your Word. Father, bless our health; bless us with a sound mind. Bless our families with reconciliation and peace.

Father, bless our cities and churches with unity. Bless our homes with safety. Bless our finances to increase, and then bless us to give back to You and to the work of Your kingdom. Father, give us a heart of compassion, desiring souls to be saved.

I pray that our spirit man will come alive. I pray that the eyes of our understanding will be opened, that You will give us wisdom and peace in every situation we are faced with. Father, bless us to be salt and light in this world.

Father, I pray that we will seek Your Face and not just Your Hand. I pray that we will develop a desire to carry out Your Will for our lives.

Father You have placed so much in our lives; help us to be able to manifest these gifts that You have given us. Lead and direct us to people that will be able to help us reach the destiny that You have pre-ordained for us.

Father, we thank You that You encourage the hearts and minds of Your people. Thank You that You love us with an everlasting love, and that You are with us. Your promise is that You will never leave nor forsake us, and Father we thank You that, that's long enough.

Father thank You that You know us and call us by name; thank You for unprecedented favor; thank You for protection and safe travel wherever we go. God, You said that we can ask for whatever we want. Your Word says if we pray according to Your Will, You hear us, and we can have the petition for what we ask. Thank You that You are our Source.

Father, we thank You because You are Great. You are Faithful.

Father, thank You for going before us, and for preparing our way. We are blessed having You on our side destroying yokes and taking care of us. Thank You for delivering Your people from hopelessness. Thank You for healing Your people from abuse and pain of all sorts ~ emotional, physical or mental.

Thank You for financial breakthrough. Thank You for miracles, signs, and wonders. Help us to grow in grace. We believe Your promise to save our children and our grandchildren.

Deliver our young people from darkness into Your marvelous Light. Deliver us from anger, unforgiveness, rebellion and destruction. Give us pure hearts and clean hands.

Thank You Jesus for 'joy unspeakable and full of glory.' Thank You for Your grace and mercy. Thank you for Your Word declares that when a man's ways are pleasing to You, even his enemies will be at peace with him.

MAY I PRAY WITH YOU?
Effective Prayer Without Ceasing

Increase our faith. Help us to grow in grace and in the knowledge of the Lord Jesus Christ. Father, bless and prosper every one of Your people; help us believe Your Word.

You declare that healing is our bread and we partake of our portion today. Thank you Lord that You will bring justice to Your elect that cry out to You day and night.

You know us by name and what we have need of. We submit everything to You. We know that You are a prayer answering God.

Thank You for life, health and strength. Father, we thank You, we praise You, we give You glory. We call everyone to You that does not know You. For those of us that do know You, Father, lift our hearts, lift our heads; lift our spirit. Father, in the name of Jesus, we bless You, we honor You, we delight in You and we celebrate You.

Father, today we bless and give You thanks for Your wonderful salvation and love in Jesus name. Amen!

CHAPTER 2

WHY PRAY?

Why breathe? To one who loves God, prayer is as natural as breathing. We pray because we live, move, and have our being in God. We breathe. Therefore, we pray. We pray because we desire to communicate with God. Prayer is two-way communication between God and you. If I am talking to you, then I am not praying; I am talking. But when I speak with God, and listen for Him to answer me back, then I am praying.

My soul prospers when I pray. It is well with my soul. If you want a soul that lives well on this earth and gets along well with others, learn to pray. Praying well is living well because praying well is a lifestyle. Prayer then is simply building your relationship with God to the point where you can communicate well with Him and He communicates well with you. *So why pray?* To live well with God and others on this side of heaven. Now is God's perfect timing for us to pray! *Because there won't be a need for prayer in His Glorious Presence on the other side. We need prayer on this side!*

"Beloved, I pray that in all respects you may prosper and be in good health, just as your soul prospers." (3 John 1:2)

"It is the blessing of the Lord that makes rich, and He adds no sorrow to it." (Proverb 10:22)

"Blessed be the God and Father of our Lord Jesus Christ, who has blessed us with every spiritual blessing in the heavenly places in Christ. Just as He chose us in Him before the foundation of the world, that we would be holy and blameless before Him in love." (Ephesians 1:3-4)

His Promise

God offers us a relationship. This relationship is filled with covenant promises. He promises that if we give ourselves to this relationship by building our souls up in Him, then His way promises us success. We communicate with God in order to build that relationship, just like we would in any healthy relationship. We observe and do the things that we understand to be good for the relationship. This is why we pray so that we can enjoy a living thriving interactive relationship with God.

"This book of the law shall not depart from your mouth, but you shall meditate on it day and night, so that you may be careful to do according to all that is written in it; for then you will make your way prosperous, and then you will have success." (Joshua 1:8)

What is Prayer?

Take up your cross daily

Prayer is communicating with God. It is connecting with Him in worship by exiting the natural realm and entering the spiritual realm. In prayer, one enters into fellowship with God on an intimate level and there is an intermingling of the knowledge and wisdom of God. Prayer involves laying down one's own will and being willing to obey God's will. In prayer, one engages in spiritual warfare. Regular praying is a lifestyle and it is an awesome way to experience the presence of God.

"Ask, and it will be given to you; seek, and you will find; knock, and it will be opened to you." (Matthew 7:7 New American Standard Bible)

"But seek first His kingdom and His righteousness,

and all these things will be added to you." (Matthew 6:33)

"Like newborn babies, long for the pure milk of the Word, so that by it you may grow in respect to salvation." (1 Peter 2:2)

So then prayer is sincere communication with God. This can include: repentance, forgiveness, adoration, worship, praise, thanksgiving, and petition.

Many references in Scripture encourage us to have a strong prayer life. The Bible tells us:

"Pray without ceasing."

(1 Thessalonians 5:17)

"Therefore, confess your sins to one another, and pray for one another so that you may be healed. The effective prayer of a righteous man can accomplish much." (James 5:16)

"And all things you ask in prayer, believing, you will receive." (Matthew 21:22)

What does Prayer do?

- Prayer gives you keys to the heavenly realms.

- Prayer causes what is happening in the spiritual realm to be manifested in the natural realm.

- Prayer increases your faith and unlocks doors.

- Prayer releases and gives authority in Jesus' name.

Jesus said, "Truly I say to you, whatever you bind on earth shall have been bound in heaven; and whatever you loose on earth shall have been loosed in heaven." (Matthew 18:18)

How do we learn to pray?

We learn to pray by praying, just as we learn to drive by driving.

- Declare a decree and it shall be! (Job 22:28)

- The Word of God guides you!

Praying God's Word is the most successful way to stop praying the problem and instead begin to pray the solution.

- Pray according to God's will. God's Word is God's will!

- Reading the Books of Psalm and Proverbs frequently can instill in your spirit a great foundation for prayer.

- Believe you will receive and you will have it!

"Therefore I say to you, all things for which you pray and ask, believe that you have received them, and they will be granted you." (Mark 11:24)

Years ago, Christians used to say: "Prayer is the key of heaven; faith unlocks the door."

Seek Him and He will hear you.

"It's well known that God isn't at the beck and call of sinners, but listens carefully to anyone who lives in reverence and does His will." (John 9:31 The Message Translation)

MY SOUL PROSPERS WHEN I PRAY
MAY I PRAY WITH YOU?
Effective Prayer Without Ceasing

CHAPTER 3

ELEMENTS OF PRAYER

Repentance

What is Repentance?

Repentance is turning away from all wrongdoing. It happens when you acknowledge or admit that you are wrong or going against God or others. In godly repentance one feels sorry for or regrets an action or intention. Repentance then allows one to change one's mind.

When you change your mind, you also change your direction or way of doing things.

How to Repent

Repentance is done by asking God and others to forgive you for whatever wrongdoing you have committed. Then it is important to stop doing that thing; don't continue to repeat that sin.

"For all have sinned and fall short of the glory of God." (Romans 3:23)

"Therefore let us also, seeing we are compassed about with so great a cloud of witnesses, lay aside every weight, and the sin which doth so easily beset us, and let us run with patience the race that is set before us, looking unto Jesus the author and perfecter of our faith...(Hebrews 12:1-2)

There are many ways to repent of your sins. There is no 'magic formula.' One way would be to pray the following or to pray something similar – whatever the Spirit speaks to your heart.

To repent of your sins, you might say:

Father God, I am sorry for offending You. Furthermore, I want no parts of that behavior again. I wish not to offend You, or anyone else. I repent of that sin, and I am sorry if that sin has affected anyone else. Father, shine Your light on any dark place in my heart and allow me to turn fully away from those open doors that lead to sin. I commit myself to You and ask You to fill those empty spaces in my heart where this sin once dwelt, in Jesus' name, Amen.

Why Repent?

Sin is a condition that separates us from God; it is an act, attitude, or state of being in opposition to God. God loved man so much that He sent His Son to give His life in exchange for man's sin. His Son died and was raised so that we could live! When I realize this spiritual truth, then I want to accept God's love. As in any loving relationship, I want to reciprocate God's love by loving God back. I love God by believing and trusting upon Him through Jesus Christ. In doing so, I bring Him joy and honor.

When you love someone, you want to refrain from doing anything that brings them dishonor. Because sin brings God dishonor, I want to turn away from practicing wrongdoing. As a way of life, I turn to God instead, who is sinless in order that I may be forgiven.

What to Repent of?

We should personally repent of anything that brings displeasure to God. No matter how long we've been saved, all of us can find at least (1) offense, hurt, or wrong habit that we are dealing with at any given time every day. Listed next is a sampling of things we encounter (sometimes on a daily basis) that we need to go to God and repent for (as often as necessary). As you browse through the list you may be surprised at some behaviors or actions that are considered sin. You might even read through the list of sins and say as the man did in Luke 18:25-26, *"Then who can be saved?"* But the good news is that Jesus told the man, *"The things which are impossible with men are possible with God."* (Luke 18:27)

The purpose of the sin list is not to judge or condemn, but that we may realize just how much sin has become a part of our world. I would admonish those who want to build a strong prayer life with God to know that we are never too high to get caught up in sin. Therefore it is important to keep an attitude of humility towards God and respect for Him so that we do not get caught up in the bondage of sin.

We cannot be effective "pray-ers" if we are participating in sin and unwilling to repent. Take a few moments to scroll through the lists on the next pages. All of these are examples of sin found in scripture. Examine yourself to see where you are in your faith concerning these things. You might find that now is a good time to turn your heart away from a particular sin area in your life, and turn your heart toward God. Draw closer to Him and become an effective prayer agent.

MAY I PRAY WITH YOU?
Effective Prayer Without Ceasing

OFFENDING GOD

Did you know that God has feelings too? If He didn't He couldn't love you! It is a sin to offend God or be involved with things that offend Him. If you want your prayers to be answered, first make sure you are not involved with anything that offends our Lord.

Remember to respect God, reverence Him, walk in consideration of how God feels. The following is not an all-inclusive list of offenses to God. Adopted from the book, 'Prayers' by Christian Word Ministries (Lexington, Kansas) and used by permission, this list will help you identify behavior that offends God in a world where offending God has become common. Most if not all of these sins are mentioned in the Bible. *The 'Prayers' book is an excellent resource on prayer and highly recommended. It can be ordered online for free or for donations at www.ChristianWord.org.*[1]

GOD HAS FEELINGS TOO!
IF HE DIDN'T, HE COULDN'T LOVE YOU!
MAY I PRAY WITH YOU?
Effective Prayer Without Ceasing

THE SIN LIST

A

- **Abase** – lower oneself before another as a god

- **Abandon** – leave one's responsibility

- **Abduct** – kidnap or hold another against their will

- **Abhor** – despise (hate) holy things; hate correction or justice

- **Abominate** – create or participate in an outrage, disgrace, scandal, ungodly, or evil act; commit an abomination

- **Abort a human life** – destroy a fetus, embryo, or unborn baby

- **Abuse** – anyone or anything

- **Accuse** – make accusations

- **Adultery** – commit adultery

- **Afflict** – others

- **Aggravate** – agitate, frustrate, or nag others

- **Aid** – or abet in crime or any wrongdoing

- **Alcoholism & Addiction** – get drunk or high

- **Act** – like you know God when you don't have a relationship with Him; participate in any unrighteous act

- **Anger** – live in anger

- **Animosity** – carry hostility in your heart

- **Anxiety** – fretfulness, nervousness, or worry

- **Apprehension** – fear or cause fear to others

- **Argumentative behavior** – to fuss; argue

- **Arrogant** – bigheaded egotistical behavior, thoughts, tone, or communication

- **Assault** – attack or strike someone

- **Astrology** – practicing horoscopes, psychic readings, tarots, etc.

- **Atheism** – not believe in God

- **Avariciousness** – greed

B

- **Backbite** – speaking badly behind someone's back

- **Backslide** – to fall back into a sinful habit

- **Bad Attitude**

- **Bad Language**

- **Bear false witness** – lie

- **Big talk** – overdo; always boasting/ bragging; or too quick to speak

- **Believe** the lies of the enemy

- **Belittle**

- **Betray** Jesus

- **Bicker**

- **Be a Bigot**, - racist, extremist or hypocrite

- **Be bitter**

- **Black Magic** – sorcery, witchcraft

- **Blackmail**

- **Blaspheme** – curse, reject, deny, or lie on the Holy Spirit, God, or Jesus

- **Boast in yourself** – be full of pride/arrogance

- **Bowing down** – to gods or serving images

- **Brag and boast** – to show off; to take claim

- **Brainwash** – to manipulate or feed people lies

- **Break commandments** of God

- **Break vows and covenants** to God or others

- **Bribe** – give or accept a bribe

- **Be brutal**; act cruel toward someone or thing

- **Burn incense** to gods

C

- **Calamity** – disaster, disarray, disorder

- **Carelessness**

- (trust in) **Cares & riches** of this world

- **Carnality** (focused on self or material things)

- **Cast God aside** or look away from God

- **Cause conflict** and disorder (does not mean differences in opinions); Creating distresses, division, and fear

- **Cause confusion**

- **Cause men to err**

- **Cause offense**

- **Cause the poor to fail**

- **Change the truth to a lie**

- **Chant of charms**

- **Cheat**

- **Come against God's anointed**

- **Commit willful and/or intentional sin**

- **Complain**

- **Complacent against God's will** – satisfied doing wrong

- **Conceit** – lies or deviousness

- **Concupiscence** – lust, sexual desire

- **Condemn the innocent** or the just

- (being) **Confrontational** when there is no need to be

- **Conjure** up stories against or conspire against

- **Conspire** against God

- **Consult psychics**, wizards, or sorcerers

- (be in) **Contempt**

- (be) **Contentious** – litigious, starting trouble

- (be) **Controlling**/manipulative

- **Connive** or plot against

- (act in) **Compulsiveness**; lack of self-control

- (create) **Contention** or strife; always fighting

- **Contesting God** – withstanding or resisting God

- (participate in) **Corruption**

- (be a) **Counterfeit** – fake person

- **Cover** up your sin

- **Covet** – (desire) anything or any person that belongs to another

- (be) **Critical**

- (be) **Crooked**

- (be) **Cruel**

- (use of) **Crystals as in occult** practices

- **Curse God**

- **Curse**

- (be) **Cynical** – pessimistic, skeptic, doubting

D

- **Deal treacherously**

- **Deceive,** be deceitful, or become deceived

- **Defame** someone or something

- (act in) **Defeatism,** negativity, or have loser mentality

- (be) **Defiant** or insubordinate; rebellious

- **Defile**

- **Degrade**

- **Deject**

- become attracted to **Demon consciousness**

- **Demon worship**

- **Deny Jesus** and His resurrection

- **Depend on others to do what you can do** for yourself

- **Depravity** - participate in (evil, immorality, corruption, wickedness)

- **Desecrate** - damage, vandalize holy vessels

- **Desires of this world** - be worldly or caught up in

- **Depressing actions** - despair and engage in

- **Despise God, His Name and His Word**

- **Despise spouse**, parents, neighbors, or others

- be full of **Despitefulness**

- be **Despondent**; act in hopelessness, misery

- **Deny the truth** - not believe God

- **Discord**

- be in **Discouragement**

- **Discredit others good name** or works

- **Disdain**

- **Disgust**

- **Dishonest**

- **Dislike the love of good men**

- **Disobey**

- **Disobey God**

- **Disorderly**

- **Dispute without cause**

- **Disregard God's work**

- **Disrespect God**

- **Disruptive**

- **Dissension**

- (being) **Distant**

- **Distrust**

- **Divining or witchcraft**

- be in **Division**

- **Divorce**

- be **Domineering** (controlling)

- **Double-talk**

- **Double-minded**

- **Doubt**

- **Dread**

- **Drive people away** from true worship

- **Drug abuse** or drunkenness

- **Duplicity** (deceit, deception, disloyalty)

- **Drink blood**

E

- **Eat blood and sin offerings**

- **Eat unclean food**

- **Effeminate** (sissy) behavior

- be full of **Egotism**

- be under **Enchantment**

- **Envy**

- **Envy produced by lust**

- **Escaping or not facing the truth**

- **Evil hearts & imaginations**

- (act in) **Exasperation,** frustration, irritation

- **Exploit** - take advantage of the Gospel message or Christian work for personal profit

- **Extort money or property**

F

- **Fail or fall off in duty**

- **Fail to glorify God**

- (bear) **False burdens**

- (bear) **False compassion**

MAY I PRAY WITH YOU?
Effective Prayer Without Ceasing

- (bear) **Falsehood**
- (bear) **False humility**
- (bear) **False praise**
- (bear) **False responsibility**
- live in **Fantasy** instead of facing the truth world
- **Fantasize** in lust, envy, or covetousness
- **Find fault**
- **Fear**
- **Fear accusation**
- **Fear condemnation**
- **Fear disapproval**
- **Fear man**
- **Fear rejection**
- **Fear failure**
- **Fear reproof**

- **Fetishes** – idol images, charms, things preoccupied with

- **Fighting**

- **Flattery**

- **Fleshliness** – preoccupation with self or things you can see, touch, taste, smell, hear, i.e. Sensuality

- **Fooling self and/or others**

- **Foolishness**

- **Following any ways of man**

- **Folly**

- **Forbidding the preaching of God's word**

- **Forcefulness**

- **Forgetting God and His work**

- **Fornication** – sex outside of marriage relationship

- **Forsaking the assembly** – neglecting the saints; not spending quality time coming together with members of the Body of Christ for worship and corporately seeking more of God's presence

- **Fortune telling**

- **Fraud**

- **Fretting**

- **Frigidity** – coldness; aloofness; not open to fellowship with others

- **Frustrations**

- **Fury** – anger, wrath, ferocity

G

- **Gendering strife** – stirring up mess

- **Giving judgment** for reward

- **Giving offense**

- **Giving others drugs or alcohol**

- **Gloominess**

- **Gluttony** – excessively taking in more than what is needed, for example, overeating

- **Gossip**

- **Greed**

- **Grieving God and the Holy Spirit** – causing God to be saddened by your sin

- **Grumbling**

- **Guilt**

H

- **Hard-hearted**

- **Harlotry** – whoredom, prostitution, 'hootchie' behavior

- **Harshness**

- **Hating God** or **Hating God's Word**

- **Hating**

- **Haughtiness** – arrogance, pride, self-worship

- **Having other gods**

- **Headiness** – having the big-head, arrogance, know-it-all

- **High-minded** – know-it-all, an un-teachable spirit, arrogant

- **Holding God's table in contempt** – attempting to punish the saints, the church, or their work

- **Homosexuality** – rejecting God-created identity by embracing sexual or intimate relations of the same sex

- **Hopelessness**

- **Horoscopes** – astrology, zodiacs

- **Human sacrifice**

- **Hypocrisy** – not living what you speak; faking

I

- **Idleness,** idle words, thoughts, deeds, & actions

- **Idols** and idolatry of any kind

- **Ignorance and ignoring God**; ignoring God's miracles

- **Ill-will**

- **Imitating true worship**

- **Inhumanity and immorality**

- **Impatience**

- **Impenitence** – not sorry for wrongdoing; non-repentant

- **Impetuousness** – flying off the handle; sudden reaction without thinking through rationally first

- **Implacability** – not wanting to be at peace or satisfied

- **Imprudence** – not using discretion; unwise

- **Impu**re thoughts or impurity

- **Incest** – intimate involvement with one in the same immediate bloodline or family

- **Incitement** – provoking

- **Indifferences** – lacks of interest or failing to be sympathetic

- **Inflating** – exaggerating

- **Inflexibility** – not willing to work through or work together

- **Inhospitality** – not greeting or being warm or friendly toward others

- **Injustice** – unfairness, biased, discriminating, prejudice

- **Inquiring of idols** – seeking or asking of others that you worship instead of God

- **Insolence** – disrespect

- **Intemperance** – over indulgent; self-indulgent

- **Intentional sins**

- **Intimidation** – bullying, pressure through fear or power, coercion

- **Intolerances** – narrow-mindedness; bigotries/prejudices

- **Intellectualism and sophistication** – high-mindedness

- **Inventing sin**

- **Inventing evil**

- **Inward wickedness**

- **Irrationality** – not being logical

- **Irreverence** – disrespect

J

- **Jealousy**

- **Being judgmental**

- **Justifying the wicked**

K

- **Kidnapping**

- **Killing**

L

- **Lack of self-control**

- **Lawlessness**

- **Lasciviousness** – lustfulness; lewd; without moral restraint

- **Laziness**

- **Legalism** – strict adherence to laws in the Bible without regard to a relationship with Jesus Christ

- **Lesbianism** – rejecting God-created identity by embracing sexual or intimate relations between females

- **Levitation** – raising in the air supernaturally

- **Lewdness** – vulgar, vile, filthy, unwholesome

- **Limiting God**

- **Lip service**

- **Living contrary to nature** – going against God's natural or spiritual laws

- **Loathing** – hating

- **Longing for sin**

- **Loneliness**

- **Loose morals**

- **Looting**

- **Loving to curse**

- **Loving evil**

- **Loving money**

- Loving to be chief

- Loving human titles

- Loving human praise

- Lust

- Lust of the eye

- Lust of the flesh

- Lust of the mind

- Laying in wait to sin

- Lying

- Lying to the Holy Spirit

- Lying with pleasure and delight

M

- Madness

- Magic

- Male prostitution

- Making or buying images

- **Making false vows**

- **Making God a liar**

- **Making war**

- **Maliciousness** – spiteful, mean, cruel

- **Manipulation** – exploiting another

- **Manslaughter**

- **Marauding** – looting

- **Masturbation** – self sexual stimulation

- **Materialism** – clinging to material things

- **Meanness**

- **Misbelieving**

- **Mischief**

- **Misery**

- **Misleading**

- **Misuse of the law**

- **Mocking**

- **Mulishness** - stubbornness

- **Murder**

- **Murmuring**

- **Murmuring** about wages

- **Muttering**

N

- **Necromancy** – communicating with the dead

- **Negativism**

- **Nervous habits**

- **Nicotine addiction**

- **Not having a conscience**

- **Not being a good steward** of your money

- **Not fearing God**

- **Not giving to the poor**

- **Not honoring fathers and mothers**

- **Not letting go of wickedness**

- **Not loving God** with all our heart, soul, and mind; not loving our neighbor as our self

- **Not loving ourselves**

- **Not observing and keeping holy the Sabbath** day

- **Not praising and worshiping God** the way we should and when we should and how we should

- **Not being watchful**

O

- **Occultism** – belief in supernatural powers in opposition to Christ as God's Supreme Power

- **Obsessing**

- **Obstinacy** – unreasonable, stubbornness

- **Offering polluted sacrifices**

- **Opposing the Gospel**

- **Oppressing widows and orphans**

- **Oppression**

- **Overbearing**

P

- **Pastors destroying and scattering people** in the church

- **Pastors destroying and misleading** people not in the church

- **Pedophilia** – adult sexual desire for a child

- **Persecuting believers**

- **Persecuting the poor**

- **Persecution**

- **Perversion** – distortion, falsifying

- **Perverting the Gospel**

- **Perverting truth** for personal gain

- **Petulance** – terrible temper

- **Planning without God**

- **Plotting**

- **Plundering** – preying upon others

- **Polluting God's house** and Sabbaths

- **Pompousness** - snobbish

- **Pornography** – obscene sexual materials

- **Possessiveness**

- **Pouting**

- **Poverty mentality**

- **Prayerlessness**

- **Prejudice**

- **Presumption** – assumptions without regard for god's thoughts or ways

- **Pretending to be a prophet**

- **Pretension** – false position; putting on airs

- **Pridefulness**

- **Pride of life**

- **Procrastination** – putting off for another time when something should be done now

- **Profane God** and His holiness

- **Profanity unto God**

- **Professing to be wise**

- **Prophecy by Baal** – statement of a false god

- **Prophesying lies**

- **Propagating lies** – spreading lies

- **Proudness**

- **Provoking God**

- **Provoking**

- **Puffing up**

Q

- **Quarreling**

- **Quenching the Holy Spirit**

- **Questioning God's Word**

R

- **Raiding**

- **Railing**

- **Raging**

- **Raping**

- **Rationalization**

- **Ravaging**

- **Rebellion**

- **Rebuking the Lord**

- **Recklessness**

- **Refusing correction**

- **Refusing to hear**

- **Refusing to repent**

- **Refusing to destroy ungodly altars**

- **Refusing to be humble**

- **Refusing to live in peace**

- **Regarding iniquity in your heart**

- **Rejecting reproof** – refusing correction

- **Rejecting salvation**

- **Rejecting God and His Word**

- **Rejection**

- **Rejoicing in others' adversity**

- **Rejoicing in idols**

- **Rejoicing in iniquity**

- **Repetitiveness**

- **Reproaching good men**

- **Requiring usury** – demanding extremely high interest or more than what's fair

- **Resentment** – anger, bitterness, hatred

- **Restlessness**

- **Retaliation** – take vengeance

- **Returning evil for good**

- **Returning hate for love**

- **Reveling**

- **Reviling**

- **Revenge**

- **Rewarding evil for good**

- **Rigidity** – firm, too strict

- **Robbing God**

- **Robbery**

- **Rudeness**

S

- **Sacrificing children** to demons

- **Sadism** – fighting brutally

- **Scheming**

- **Scornfulness** - disrespect

- **Scorning religion** –disrespect for the sacred

- **Seduction** – sexual enticement

- **Seeking self gain**

- **Seeking pleasures of this world**

- **Seizing in an evil way**

- **Self-accusations**

- **Self-admiration**

- **Self-centeredness**

- **Self-condemnation**

- **Self-corruption**

- **Self-criticalness**

- **Self-deception** – lying to yourself

- **Self-delusion** – fooling yourself

- **Self-destruction**

- **Self-exultation** – praising yourself

- **Self-glorification** – worshipping self

- **Self-hatred**

- **Self-importance**

- **Self-rejection**

- **Selfishness**

- **Self-pity**

- **Self-righteousness** – self salvation; being right on one's own without God

- **Self-seeking**

- **Self-will**

- **Serving other gods**

- **Setting aside Godly counsel**

- **Setting heart to sin**

- **Sewing discord**

- **Sexual idolatry**

- **Sexual immorality**

- **Sexual impurity**

- **Sexual lewdness**

- **Sexual perversion**

- **Sodomy** – anal intercourse between two men, or sexual intercourse involving people and animals

- **Shame**

- **Shamelessness**

- **Silliness or stupidity** (as in foolishness)

- **Sin consciousness**

- **Sinful mirth** – amusement with sin

- **Sissyness**

- **Skepticism** – doubt, uncertainty, no faith

- **Slander** – insult, smear, defame someone

- **Slaughter**

- **Slaying**

- **Slothfulness** – non-caring lateness, slowness

- **Snobbishness**

- **Soothsaying** – predicting of the ungodly

- **Sorcery** – wizardry and witchcraft

- **Sowing seeds of hatred**

- **Speaking curses**

- **Speaking incantations** – casting spells, charms

- **Speaking folly**

- **Speculation** – not talking what you know but rather what you guess

- **Spell-casting**

- **Spiritual laziness**

- **Spitefulness**

- **Stealing**

- **Stiff-necked**

- **Strife**

- **Striving over leadership**

- **Struggling**

- **Stubbornness**

- **Stupidity**

- **Suicidal thoughts**

- **Suspicion**

- Swallowing up the needy

- Swearing to false gods

- Swearing

T

- Taking **advantage** of others

- Taking a bribe

- Taking offense

- Taking God's name in vain

- Taking **rights away** from the poor

- Teaching and tolerating wickedness

- Teaching false doctrines

- Temper

- Temptation

- Tempting God

- Theft

- Threatening disaster

- **Timidity**
- **Tolerating false** prophets
- **Tolerating sin** and its ways
- **Tolerating wicked** men
- **Trafficking with demons**
- **Trickery**
- **Two-facedness**
- **Trusting lies**
- **Trusting our own beauty**
- **Trusting in our own righteousness**
- **Trusting wickedness**
- **Tumults** – stirring up; noisy disturbance
- **Turning to folly**
- **Turning aside the way of the meek**
- **Turning your back on God**
- **Turning from righteousness**

- **Turning aside for money**

U

- **Unbelief**

- **Unbridled lust**

- **Uncleanness**

- **Uncompromising**

- **Undermining**

- **Unequally yoked to non-believers**

- **Unfairness**

- **Unfaithfulness in trust**

- **Unfaithfulness**

- **Unforgiveness**

- **Unfriendliness**

- (enter into) **Ungodly soul ties**

- (enter into) **Unrighteous agreements**

- **Ungratefulness**

- **Unholy alliances**

- **Unholy habits**

- **Unmanly**

- **Unmercifulness**

- **Unreadiness**

- **Unrepenting**

- **Unrighteousness of laws**

- **Unrighteousness**

- **Unruliness of tongues**

- **Unsparing**

- **Un-submissiveness**

- **Unthankfulness**

- **Untruthfulness**

- (being) **Unwise**

- **Unworthiness**

- **Using tarot cards**

V

- **Vain imaginations**
- **Vain repetitions**
- **Vanity**
- **Vengeance**
- **Viciousness**
- **Vile affections** – loving evil
- **Vile speaking** – evil talk
- **Violence**
- **Vulgarity**

W

- **Walking after our own devices**
- **Walking for unprofitable things**
- **Walking after our own thoughts**
- **Walking after false gods**
- **Walking with sinners**

- **Water witching** – witchcraft using water

- **White magic**

- **Wickedness**

- **Willful sin**

- **Willful blindness to the truth**

- **Winking with evil intent**

- **Witchcraft**

- **Withdrawal**

- **Withholding a pledge**

- **Without concern for others**

- **Without natural affection**

- **Without mercy**

- **Workaholic**

- **Working iniquity**

- **Working for praise**

- **Worldliness**

- **Worrying**

- **Worshipping false gods**, possessions, or worshipping our work(s)

- **Worshipping the creation** instead of the Creator

- **Worshipping planets**

- **Wrath in one's heart or on one's mind**

- **Wrong doing**

Z

- **Zealousness to make others sin**

- **Zealousness in outward show**

THE GOOD NEWS

We are reminded that Jesus came to deliver us from not just the sins on the Sin List, but **ALL SIN** – including the condition or state of being sinful.

There is only one word perfect enough to get rid of sin: **LOVE**.

John 3:16-18 (KJV)

MAY I PRAY WITH YOU?
Effective Prayer Without Ceasing

16 For God so loved the world, that he gave his only begotten Son, that whosoever believeth in him should not perish, but have everlasting life.

17 For God sent not his Son into the world to condemn the world; but that the world through him might be saved.

18 He that believeth on him is not condemned: but he that believeth not is condemned already, because he hath not believed in the name of the only begotten Son of God.

REMEMBER: The Bible says that we are *in this world* but not *of this world*. God has not given us the spirit of fear nor bondage to sin! Therefore, do not allow yourself to be in bondage to any sin – instead go to God in prayer! As sons and daughters who trust and believe on Christ Jesus, then we can go to God just as we would go to a loving Daddy and ask Him to make us whole (Romans 8:15).

When you repent, focus on loving God with all your heart, all of your mind, and all your strength, **and** focus on loving others the same way. This is the kind of love God gives us; it's greater than any one of our sins, including the sins you noticed on the Sin List.

Repentance and forgiveness is the key to opening God's heart. Let God make you whole! If we love God and love our fellow man, the Bible says that we would not be open to living a life of sin. Therefore, we are to love God, love ourselves, and love our fellow man. This includes having an attitude of forgiveness and repentance for any wrongs done. This kind of love shows that we are God's people and He is our God. Upon this one statement: *Love God and love others as you love yourself* rests all the laws of the prophets and the entire Bible! (Matthew 22:40)

"By this all men will know that you are My disciples, if you have love for one another." (John 13:35)

If we confess our sins, he is faithful and righteous to forgive us our sins and to cleanse us from all unrighteousness." (1 John 1:9)

 "And if My people who are called by My name humble themselves and pray and seek My face and turn from their wicked ways, then will I hear from heaven, will forgive their sin and will heal their land." (2 Chronicles 7:14)

"For you have not received a spirit of slavery leading to fear again, but you have received a spirit of

adoption as sons by which we cry out, 'Abba, Father!'"
(Romans 8:15)

Renunciation

Renunciation is to take a stand against the things that God hates. It is to set oneself in agreement with God against the very same thing that God is in disagreement with.

God had a very clear agenda in the world; it was to show and define for man what is love through the person of Jesus Christ, Emmanuel, meaning *God with us.* In doing so, God showed Himself a loving father to sons and daughters of His creation. Anything that would bring harm, separation, or exile (physically or spiritually) between God and His sons and daughters – this is what God hates.

To renounce is to:

- Formally declare one's abandonment

- Refuse to recognize or abide by any longer

- Declare that one will no longer engage in or support

- Reject or stop using or consuming.

EX: You could state: Lord, I completely renounce:

- Drugs

- Alcohol

- Nicotine

- Pornography

- Lying

- Stealing,...whatever your vice may be

Once you renounce sins and anything that may present to hinder your life, you must stay out of and away from the sources of those pitfalls, such as: drug dealers or places where drugs are available; bars or places that serve alcohol; pornographic material or web sites; stop purchasing nicotine; choose to speak truth; choose to obtain your own possessions, etc. Almost daily I renounce something from my life:

- Anger

- Fear

- Worry

You fill in the blanks for your life!

Why Renounce?

It is necessary to know where you stand in your own heart on the person of Jesus Christ. Renounce anything that sets itself against knowing and experiencing the revelation and love of Jesus Christ for yourself. One blatant example of rejecting God in the form of rejecting the love and revelation of Jesus Christ is the practice of cults. That would include experience with all cults, occults and all their practices because these groups tend to acknowledge and promote hatred of Jesus and rebellion against God.

It is possible to experience God personally, His character, His ways, and His love for you through trusting and believing on Jesus Christ. The more you seek to know Jesus and experience the true love of Jesus Christ, the more you become drawn and attracted to God the Father. Conversely, the more one rejects the thought of Jesus Christ and His love, His life, His death, burial, and resurrection, the more resistant one becomes to anything God has spoken or done. These types of activities against Christ can be referred to as "anti" Jesus or anti-Christ.

Many who participate in 'anti-Jesus' or 'anti-Christ' groups and activities are not aware that these groups deny the revealing power of God's love. They either reject in part or in total the life, death, burial, and resurrection of Jesus Christ as God's only substitute for their sin. If you or someone you know has rejected Jesus Christ in this manner, you might cry out to God for the true revelation of who Christ is. You could start by praying: God, I renounce all cults, occults and all similar practices that deny the life, love, liberty, and legacy of Jesus Christ as my Lord and Savior who gave Himself that I might live free of the bondage of enmity and ignorance against God.

According to Bob Larson, who studied cults in over 70 countries, an estimated 1,500 to 3,000 cult groups flourish in North American society. [2] All cults have one thing in common; they consider Jesus Christ to be optional, not essential to a relationship with God.

Some major cults include:

- Hinduism

- Buddhism

- Islam

- Christian Science

- Scientology

MAY I PRAY WITH YOU?
Effective Prayer Without Ceasing

- Jehovah's Witnesses

- Mormonism

- Armstrongism

- Astrology

- Baha'ism

- New Age

- Hare Krishna

If you have participated in any such group, or have believed in any cult concept such as reincarnation, hypnosis, séances; or have meditated on anything other than the Word of God, it would be wise to renounce it all. You could simply say out loud or within your heart,

"Father, I renounce involvement with..."

You fill in the blank for your life!

Tell God how much you hate the thought of participating in or giving yourself to worship, praise, rely upon, or adore anything or anyone outside of Him. Then tell God how you feel about Him. You can literally say to God what you think about Him. You could tell God what the scriptures say about Him. For example, you could tell Him...*You are sovereign. You are wonderful. You are magnificent. You are kind. You are supreme. You are loving. You are worthy. You are marvelous. You are righteous. You are holy. You are my creator, sustainer, provider, source, and my soon coming King! Hallelujah!*

Asking for and Providing Forgiveness

We cannot do anything effective for God with unforgiveness in our heart. That includes praying. The Bible says a lot more about forgiveness than it says about many other subjects.

"Blessed are the peacemakers, for they shall be called sons of God." (Matthew 5:9)

"Whenever you stand praying, forgive, if you have anything against anyone, so that your Father who is in heaven will also forgive you your transgressions." (Mark 11:25)

"And forgive us our debts, as we also have forgiven our debtors...For if you forgive others their transgressions, your heavenly Father will also forgive you. But if you do not forgive others, then your Father will not forgive your transgressions."

(Matthew 6:12; 14-15)

"If your brother sins, go and show him his fault in private; if he listens to you, you have won your brother." (Matthew 18:15)

Let us never confuse hurts with unforgiveness. One writer said, "hurting people -- hurt people!" Hurts can be healed; however, forgiveness requires confession and repentance.

(See important scriptures and aspects of forgiveness in the Prayer Tips section under the heading: Keys to Effective Prayer.)

Sometimes in the midst of asking people to forgive us, they reject us instead. Although rejection on any level can be a very painful experience, know that many times when people reject us or push us out of their lives, their exit from our lives enables us to seek God without distraction and move to the next step toward our divine destiny in God.

"The secret of the LORD is for those who fear Him; And He will make them know His covenant." (Psalm 25:14)

Worship

Worship our Father by speaking, singing, or expressing love, adoration and appreciation directly to Him not to others. You might say to the Lord, *"I honor You; I bless You, and I delight in You. I glorify Your name. I love You; I worship You."*

You may worship the Lord through song. Select a song that magnifies God – a song that makes God larger than any circumstance you might be facing. Revisit a song possibly from your childhood that spoke about the greatness of God and about His unconditional love for you.

Although worship may stir up emotions, it is much more than an emotional experience. Worship is an intimate experience. It is opening yourself up to God expressing yourself in a most transparent way, allowing God to come and fill your presence with His presence.

Worship is not just singing or speaking words, worship is any intimate expression of who God is to you. Therefore, worship is a personal experience. You make it a lifestyle. For you, that might be any deliberate action expressing your reverence to God. I might worship God in my thinking, painting, dancing, writing, or crying. One might think of worship as something I can only do with God alone – even if others are in the room. The worship experience is between God and me.

Praise

If worship is between God and me, then praise is something I can do with others. It is me affirming and commending God before others, offering an expression of how good, great, and wonderful God is.

"I will bless the LORD at all times; His praise shall continually be in my mouth." (Psalm 34:1)

"Praise the LORD! For it is good to sing praises to our God; For it is pleasant and praise is becoming." (Psalm 147:1)

"Let everything that has breath praise the Lord. Praise the Lord!" (Psalm 150:6)

"From the rising of the sun to its setting, the name of the LORD is to be praised." (Psalm 113:3 NAS)

Petitions

Petitions are requests we ask of God. We bring our concerns and desires to Him just as we would discuss things with our best friends and loved ones. We seek the people we love for support and guidance in our daily affairs; it is the same with God, but even more important since He is our source.

"This is the confidence which we have before Him, that, if we ask anything according to His will, He hears us. And if we know that He hears us in whatever we ask, we know that we have the requests which we have asked from Him." (1 John 5: 14-15)

God's Word is His will.

"For we through the Spirit, by faith, are waiting for the hope of righteousness." (Galatians 5:5)

"If My people who are called by My name humble themselves and pray and seek My face and turn from their wicked ways, then I will hear from heaven, will forgive their sin and will heal their land." (2 Chronicles 7:14)

"Therefore He is able also to save forever those who draw near to God through Him, since He always lives to make intercession for them." (Hebrews 7:25)

ELEMENTS OF PRAYER

Fasting

Fasting is abstaining from food or sometimes other pleasures, such as television, sports, music, etc. in order to spend focused time with God. Fasting can be done for multiple reasons, including medical, dieting, and most importantly, seeking a God-focused life. In fasting, the focus is not abstaining from food or things we give up, but rather the focus is on developing a connection with God – the kind of connection that results in righteous living, peace, and joy from having spent time with Him. *For the kingdom of God is not meat and drink, but righteousness, peace, and joy in the Holy Spirit* (Romans 14:17).

Fasting helps take our minds off of ourselves and having things our way to instead focus our attention on God's way. Fasting disciplines us and causes us to pray and seek God for a closer relationship with Him. When we fast, we are motivated to spend more time with God as we experience breakthrough communication with the Lord. Breakthrough communication can come in the form of a word from the Lord or a sign; it can also come in the form of guidance, peace in our thoughts and mind, and contentment in our hearts that was not there before. Fasting takes the focus off of us and places it on the things of God because we come to a point in the fast where we begin to trust God and rely on Him through constantly communicating in prayer and seeking to hear, understand, and depend upon Him more.

The sacrifice that we make by focusing on God in fasting is rewarded by a closer more tangible relationship with the Lord, Jesus Christ. We actually begin to recognize His presence around us. There is a sense of knowing that He is there, and His presence brings us peace of mind.

Not only does prayer and fasting bring about greater peace of mind, Jesus said that some things only come through fasting and prayer! The purpose of fasting and prayer is to get results – the kingdom way – by focusing on God and not on ourselves!

"But this kind does not go out except by prayer and fasting." (Matthew 17:21)

≈≈The Prophet Daniel fasted:

"I did not eat any tasty food, nor did meat or wine enter my mouth, nor did I use any ointment at all until the entire three weeks were completed." (Daniel 10:3)

"Is this not the fast which I choose, to loosen the bonds of wickedness, to undo the bands of the yoke, and to let the oppressed go free and break every yoke? " (Isaiah 58:6)

≈≈Queen Esther called a fast:

"Go, assemble all the Jews who are found in Susa, and fast for me; do not eat or drink for three days, night or day. I and my maidens also will fast in the same way. And thus I will go in to the king, which is not according to the law; and if I perish, I perish." (Esther 4:16)

≈≈Saul fasted before his name became Paul:

"And he was three days without sight, and neither ate nor drank." (Acts 9:9)

Appearance When Fasting

Do not neglect your appearance when fasting. Such neglect does not honor God; rather it is a distraction to the purpose of your fast. Maintain your normal presentation.

"Whenever you fast, do not put on a gloomy face as the hypocrites do, for they neglect their appearance so that they will be noticed by men when they are fasting. Truly I say to you, they have their reward in full." (Matthew 6:16)

Tips While Fasting

It is not necessary to announce your fast to others. A fast should be a quiet set aside special time between you and God. Spouses however need to consult with one another to 'agree' on a fast.

Should you happen to 'break' your fast before the defined time period, don't use that as an excuse to cancel your fast. You will be presented with all types of distractions to hinder you from fasting. Simply continue to spend time with God, seek forgiveness, and resume or restart your fast.

Fasting is not only for your benefit, it can benefit others connected to you as when Esther, Daniel, and Jesus fasted. It is a sacred occasion where you have purposed to seek God's presence in a very personal way. As a result, a stronger connection is established between you and God in two-way communication. Various benefits include greater wisdom, knowledge, and understanding from God on a particular issue, as well as experiencing a greater awareness of forgiveness, righteousness, peace, strength, and joy, despite what may be going on around you.

CHAPTER 4

ORDER OF PRAYER

Steps to Prayer

1. Repentance

"We know that God does not hear sinners; but if anyone is God-fearing and does His will, He hears him." (John 9:31)

"I tell you, Nay: but, except ye repent, ye shall all in like manner perish." (Luke 13:3)

2. Confession

"He who conceals his transgressions will not prosper, but he who confesses and forsakes them will find compassion." (Proverbs 28:13)

"If we confess our sins, He is faithful and righteous to forgive us our sins and to cleanse us from all righteousness." (1 John 1:9)

3. Worship

"God is a spirit, and those who worship Him must worship in spirit and truth." (John 4:24)

Regardless of what's going on, God is still God, and He is worthy of worship.

4. Adoration

"O God, You are my God; I shall seek You earnestly; my soul thirsts for You, my flesh yearns for You, in a dry and weary land where there is no water." (Psalm 63:1)

Tell God who His word says He is and love on Him.

5. Praise and Thanksgiving

"Enter His gates with thanksgiving and His courts with praise. Give thanks to Him, bless His name." (Psalm 100:4)

"Rejoice always; pray without ceasing; in everything give thanks: for this is the will of God in Christ Jesus to you-ward." (1 Thessalonians 5:16-18)

6. Petition

When we petition God, it does not mean that we bring our shopping list, or that we beg out of desperation. When we petition God, we pray asking for specifics and we believe that He hears and answers us. Even if we do not see the physical manifestation of the things we ask yet, we first believe knowing that God hears us and answers our prayers – even before we ask!

Your Father knows you need things.

"Therefore I say to you, all things for which you pray and ask, believe that you have received them, and they will be granted you." (Mark 11:24)

"For this child I prayed; and Jehovah hath given me my petition which I asked of him..." (1 Samuel 1:27)

"And the king said unto Esther at the banquet of wine, What is thy petition? and it shall be granted thee: and what is thy request? Then answered Esther, and said, My petition and my request is: if I have found favor in the sight of the king, and if it please the king to grant my petition, and to perform my request..." (Esther 5:6-8)

Prayer Scriptures to Empower You

When learning to pray, start by praying scripture. Make this a lifelong habit; it is investing in you! Review and make these scripture passages your own by reading them often and applying them to your daily activities. Replace the words, "I, my, thee or thou" in these scriptures with your name:

- Psalm 23

- Psalm 34:1-7

- Psalm 91

- Psalm 139:1-4

"But seek first His kingdom and His righteousness, and all these things shall be added to you." (Matthew 6:33)

We can pray in the shower, in our car, or on our job. We can absolutely pray at all times. The words of prayer don't always have to be audibly spoken – our spirit can pray to God, even while we are talking with others.

CHAPTER 5

THE HOLY SPIRIT'S ROLE IN PRAYER

The Holy Spirit is God and God in us

The Holy Spirit perfects all things concerning us. He is God working in us and through us. He is given to all who believe and receive Him.

We are to talk with and engage the Holy Spirit in prayer because the Holy Spirit is God Himself. He is God in Spirit form. Therefore when we talk to God, we are speaking with the Holy Spirit. For example, after we have asked for forgiveness in prayer, we ought to say, "Thank you, Holy Spirit for your forgiveness." We can also say things like, "We are desperate for your presence, Holy Spirit." "We invite, invoke, and welcome you into our lives, into our midst, Holy Spirit."

When Jesus was on earth, He was here to bring us truth and set us free by leaving us His Spirit, the Holy Spirit.

As we pray, the Holy Spirit helps us develop a hunger and thirst for:

- God's Presence

- Righteousness

- Wholesome relationships

- God's Word

- Excellence

- Power

"Peter said to them, "Repent, and each of you be baptized in the name of Jesus Christ for the forgiveness of your sins; and you will receive the gift of the Holy Spirit." (Acts 2:38)

Repent, be baptized, and receive.

Receiving the Holy Spirit is a Sovereign Act of God.

"And suddenly there came from heaven a noise like a violent rushing wind, and it filled the whole house where they were sitting. And there appeared to them tongues as of fire distributing themselves, and they rested on each one of them. And they were all filled with the Holy Spirit and began to speak with other tongues, as the Spirit was giving them utterance." (Acts 2:2-4)

The Spirit gives gifts from God as He wills.

"Now when the apostles in Jerusalem heard that Samaria had received the Word of God, they sent them Peter and John, who came down and prayed for them that they might receive the Holy Spirit. For He (*The Holy Spirit*) had not yet fallen upon any of them; they had simply been baptized in the name of the Lord Jesus. Then they (*Peter and John*) began laying their hands on them, and they were receiving the Holy Spirit. Now when Simon saw that the Spirit was bestowed through the laying on of the apostles' hands, he offered them money, saying, "Give this authority to me as well, so that everyone on whom I lay my hands may receive the Holy Spirit. But Peter said to him, "May your silver perish with you, because you thought you could obtain the gift of God with money!" (Acts 8:14-20 Revised Standard Version)

The Holy Spirit cannot be bought or manipulated; He is God. He is *received* into the hearts of men.

His purpose is to keep us for Jesus until the day when Jesus returns to earth. He also gives gifts to help us on earth. We receive Him by asking and believing upon Jesus as Lord and Savior of our lives.

The Holy Spirit is not an "it;" the Holy Spirit is God Himself in Spirit form, just like Jesus is God Himself in man form.

What does Holy Spirit do?

He Speaks

"While they were ministering to the Lord and fasting, the Holy Spirit said, "Set apart for Me Barnabas and Saul for the work to which I have called them." (Acts 13:2)

He Works

"But one and the same Spirit works all these things, distributing to each one individually just as He wills." (1 Corinthians 12:11)

He Teaches

"But the Helper, the Holy Spirit, whom the Father will send in My name, He will teach you all things, and bring to your remembrance all that I, said to you." (John 14:26)

He Guides

"But when He, the Spirit of truth, comes, He will guide you into all the truth; for He will not speak on His own initiative, but whatever He hears, He will speak; and He will disclose to you what is to come." (John 16:13)

He Prays

The Holy Spirit prays for us in God's language.

"In the same way the Spirit also helps our weakness; for we do not know how to pray as we should, but the Spirit Himself intercedes for us with groaning too deep for words; and He Who searches the hearts knows what the mind of the Spirit is, because He intercedes for the saints according to the will of God." (Romans 8:26-27)

He is a Gift

"If you then, being evil, know how to give good gifts to your children, how much more will your heavenly Father give the Holy Spirit to those who ask Him?" (Luke 11:13)

We must want or desire Him.

CHAPTER 6

PRAYER TIPS

Some people are fearful or embarrassed to pray aloud or publicly. To overcome that problem, talk to God as you would talk to a very dear friend.

The way to learn to pray is by praying. Just start praying! You open your mouth and say the words.

Some say I cannot pray like others. It is not necessary to sound like or pray like anyone else; be yourself.

Practice praying. If you are speaking to God, you *are* actually praying to Him, worshipping Him, praising Him or acknowledging Him in some way. Tell God what is on your heart. In other words, tell Him about the things which concern you. Tell Him about the things that you think, like, feel, wonder, desire, don't understand, hope for, look forward to, plan to, are surprised by, etc.

Pray aloud for anyone or anything that concerns you, your family, associates, and the world around you. Pray for others in other countries, nations, and pray for industries, technologies, the arts, and sciences. You can pray for governments, families, education, media, business, and church. You can pray to God about anything and everything.

Jesus taught His disciples to pray:

"After this manner therefore pray ye. Our Father who art in heaven, Hallowed be thy name. Thy kingdom come. Thy will be done, as in heaven, so on earth. Give us this day our daily bread. And forgive us our debts, as we also have forgiven our debtors. And bring us not into temptation, but deliver us from the evil one." (Matthew 6:9-13)

Pray the words that are in the scriptures. Start with Psalm 23rd chapter and Psalm 91st chapter and insert your name where it says, "I" or "you."

For example, say, *"The Lord is Carrie's shepherd; Carrie shall not want..."* Simply open your mouth and release the words. Remember, this is how God did it when He created the universe. He opened up His mouth and spoke it into existence by faith in Himself! The Bible says that God could find none greater than

Himself, so He swore by His own name because His name was the greatest (Hebrews 6:13-18). God spoke by faith in Himself! There is none greater than God! We live and love Him all by faith.

"We walk by faith, not by sight." (2 Corinthians 5:7)

Hindrances to Prayer

Any sin condition or sinful situations – regardless of who is at fault – can hinder or prevent our prayers from being answered or acknowledged by God. Everyone sins and falls short of the perfection of God. This is why it is extremely important to keep a humble attitude before God, an attitude of forgiveness, recognizing that He is the only Holy One. We are His offspring through believing and trusting upon Jesus Christ. This makes our spirit man a perfect being to God.

Though our spirits are made perfect through Jesus Christ, we still have issues down here on earth. Our mind, will, emotions, intellect, imaginations, and desires still struggle at times with sin, and this is why we need the Holy Spirit. He is the Keeper down here on earth to help us overcome any sin as long as we allow Him to. When we fail to allow the Holy Spirit to lead, guide, and direct our paths, sin is the result.

See the Sin List in the section on Repentance for just some examples. We should not expect our prayers to be answered if we have an attitude of:

- Disregard or disrespect for the Holy Spirit

- Unconfessed sin

- Disobedience to God's Word

- Unforgiveness

- Selfish motives

Keys to Effective Prayer

Not only do we sometimes experience hindrances to prayer through sin, other common struggles with praying include:

- Praying out loud

- Praying in front of others

- Feeling like we don't know what to pray

- Not knowing God's will or scripture

- Feeling fear, guilt, shame before God

If these are challenges for you, here are some keys to help you develop a more effective life in God through prayer.

Faith

- When you pray, examine your faith in Christ

Relationship with God through Jesus Christ, seeking to know Jesus – and more of Him – is the genuine faith that moves God.

"But without faith it is impossible to please him: for he that cometh to God must believe that he is, and that he is a rewarder of them that diligently seek him." (Hebrews 11:5-7)

Wisdom

- When you pray, ask God for wisdom

"But if any of you lacks wisdom, let him ask of God who gives to all generously and without reproach, and it will be given to him." (James 1:5)

"Trust in the Lord with all your heart and do not lean on your own understanding. In all your ways acknowledge Him and He will make your paths straight." (Proverbs 3:5-6)

Encouragement

- When you pray, be encouraged

"Only be strong and very courageous; be careful to do according to all the law which Moses My servant commanded you; do not turn from it to the right or to the left, so that you may have success wherever you go." (Joshua 1:7)

Forgiveness and Repentance

- Before you pray, be forgiving of others

- Before you pray, examine your heart

"Therefore if you bring your gift to the altar, and there remember that your brother has something against you, leave your gift there before the altar, and go your way. First be reconciled to your brother, and then come and offer your gift." (Matthew 5:23 NKJV)

- Unforgiveness puts you in prison with the person that you refuse to forgive

- If we refuse to forgive we cannot, do not, will not grow in grace and in the knowledge of our Lord.

- Jesus directs us to 'forgive much' as He has forgiven much!

"Whenever you pray, forgive if you have anything against anyone, so that your Father who is in heaven will also forgive your transgressions. But if you do not forgive, neither will your Father who is in heaven forgive your transgressions." (Mark 11:25-26)

"...Lord, how often shall my brother sin against me and I forgive him? Up to seven times?" Jesus said to him, "I do not say to you, up to seven times, but up to seventy times seven." (Matthew 18:21-22)

"...And why beholdest thou the mote that is in thy brother's eye, but considerest not the beam that is in thine own eye? Or how wilt thou say to thy brother, Let me cast out the mote out of thine eye; and lo, the beam is in thine own eye?" (Matthew 7:2-4)

CHAPTER 7

TYPES OF PRAYERS

Here are a few prayers that you can refer to from time to time:

Prayer of Declaration - Declaring & Decreeing

"You will also decree a thing, and it will be established for you; and light will shine on your ways." (Job 22:28)

"Father, in Jesus' Name, in each situation that we are faced with, we thank You, that You will grant our requests according to Your Word and Will.

Father I thank You for Your faithfulness. You know what we need before we ask and it's Your good pleasure to give us the Kingdom.

I pray that Your Kingdom come and Your Will be done on earth as it is in heaven; for us, in us; through us; today, in Jesus Name."

I Declare and Decree:

- My body is totally healed

- Our sons, daughters, grand and great-grand children are saved, delivered and serving our Lord, Jesus Christ.

- Marriages are healed

- Bills are paid off

- Financial increase

- Profitable positions

- Better jobs - promotions

- Homes saved from foreclosures

- Mental health healed

- Traveling mercies

- Peace, healed hearts and emotions

- Surrendered hearts and obedience to God

Prayer of Faith

"Now faith is the assurance of things hoped for, the conviction of things not seen." (Hebrews 11:1)

"Truly I say to you, whoever says to this mountain, 'Be taken up and cast into the sea,' and does not doubt in his heart, but believes that what he says is going to happen, it will be granted to him." (Mark 11:23)

"Father, I thank You that You hear and answer my prayers. By faith in Your Word, I know that if I pray according to Your Will, You will grant my petition. Your Word declares that Faith is the substance of things hoped for and the evidence of things not seen, (Hebrews 11:1), so even if I don't see the answer; faith says it is done!"

Prayer of Thanksgiving

"Enter His gates with thanksgiving *and* His courts with praise. Give thanks to Him, bless His name. For the LORD is good; His loving-kindness is everlasting. And His faithfulness to all generations." (Psalm 100:4-5)

- We pray because we are thankful, and because His truth, loving-kindness, and faithfulness lasts throughout all generations.

- You cannot pray effectively if you are not thankful! It is because you are thankful that you come to pray because you know you have access to God.

"Father, I thank You today for I know that You hear me and You answer prayer. Thank You for Your faithfulness. Your Word says that You promised to never leave us nor forsake us. Thank You for being our God."

Prayer of Repentance

"And Peter said unto them, Repent ye, and be baptized every one of you in the name of Jesus Christ unto the remission of your sins; and ye shall receive the gift of the Holy Spirit." (Acts 2:38)

"Repent ye therefore, and turn again, that your sins may be blotted out, that so there may come seasons of refreshing from the presence of the Lord..." (Acts 3:19)

"The Lord is not slack concerning his promise, as some count slackness; but is longsuffering to you-ward, not wishing that any should perish, but that all should come to repentance." (2 Peter 3:9)

"Please forgive me Lord for (you fill in the blank ~ be specific; ask the Holy Spirit to show you if you don't

know) *that which prevents me from knowing Christ more, and making Christ known to the world by my actions of love and obedience to You."*

Prayer of Comfort in Loss of Loved Ones

"Blessed be the God and Father of our Lord Jesus Christ, the Father of mercies and God of all comfort; who comforts us in all afflictions, that we may be able to comfort those in any affliction, through the comfort wherewith we ourselves are comforted of God." (2 Corinthians 1:3-4)

"Father God, only You can fill the empty places of loss of our loved ones. Thank You for being the God of all comfort. Father with the same comfort that you have comforted me, I freely pray comfort and encouragement and healing for others."

Prayer of Intercession

A Word About Intercession

Praying as an intercessor or as 'one who stands in the gap,' we can pray directly to Jesus as a mediator on behalf of someone else.

"Therefore I exhort first of all that supplications, prayers, intercessions, and giving of thanks be made for all men..." (1 Timothy 2:1 NKJV)

Intercession moves the heart of God. Therefore, intercessors ask, seek and knock out of their love and concern for others.

- We can pray as a person who understands the cause, and the case and concern of a situation.

- We can pray as a person that identifies with someone else's pain or struggle.

"Bear one another's burdens, and thereby fulfill the law of Christ." (Galatians 6:2)

One does not have to be in an official position or office of an intercessor in order to pray for another person. However, if one does hold the position or office of an intercessor, for example within a church or ministry, keep in mind that an intercessor's character should be:

- Dependable

- Honest

- Punctual

- Respectful

- Peace Makers

- Persons of Integrity

Jesus, The Holy Spirit, and people throughout the ages have interceded on our behalf.

"He saw that there was no man, and wondered that there was no intercessor; therefore His own arm brought salvation for Him; and His own righteousness, it sustained Him." (Isaiah 59:16 NKJV)

As an intercessor, you can review these scripture passages as you pray on behalf of others:

- Romans 8: 26, 27, 34

- Hebrews 7:25

Types of Intercession

Mercy

One who intercedes for people, not fully knowing all of the circumstances.

Example: You may see and hear a fire truck or ambulance siren, you begin to pray for the safety and salvation of the people involved. You begin asking God to send someone to their aid quickly (even before the, "First Responders" arrive).

Personal

One who may have been requested to pray for a specific need. One who may routinely pray for a specific person and their needs. One who maintains integrity and confidentiality regarding the prayer needs and requests of others.

Prophetic

One who hears what the person requesting prayer is saying, however the Intercessor is actually hearing and seeing what that person is, 'not saying'. This is done by the Spirit of the Lord, speaking to the Intercessor. The Intercessor then begins to pray to God that which the Spirit of the Lord just spoke to them.

Warfare

By the Spirit of the Lord, one who commands the demonic powers to flee from persons or situations. One who by the Spirit of the Lord, cancels generational curses. One who does battle in the heavenlies for a particular situation.

Financial

One who believes and prays God's Word which says that He is able to supply all of our needs according to His riches. One who prays His Word back to Him.

We are all called to intercede for one another. Pray believing God's Word that says,

"Now to Him who is able to do exceedingly abundantly above all that we ask or think, according to the power that works in us…" (Ephesians 3:20 New King James Version)

Example of an Intercessory Prayer

"Father, I lift _____ before You, agonizing on _____'s behalf, asking You Father to deliver _____ from the spirit of depression. I stand in the gap for _____, asking You to deliver _____ from sadness and this evil darkness that is trying to overtake her. I ask Father that You free _____ from the spirits of grief and un-forgiveness and set _____ free in You. I ask Father that You give _____ the spirit of Joy in place of sadness, in Jesus name. Amen.

Prayer of Assurance

"And we know that all things work together for good to them that love God, to them who are the called according to his purpose." (Romans 8:28 King James Version)

"Father, in Jesus name I am confident of this very thing that You Who began a good work in me is faithful to complete it until the day of Christ Jesus.

I thank You Father, that You are supplying my needs according to Your riches; not my job, not my business, not my family. I rejoice because You are my Source.

Father, thank You for giving Your angels charge over me to keep me daily. I thank You Father, that I can do all things through You; Who strengthens me.

Father, thank You for Your blessings that make rich and You add no sorrow to it. Hallelujah!

Father, I thank You, that when we pray according to Your will, You will hear us and if You hear us we have the petition for which we ask. *Your Word is Your will. Help us to continue to pray Your promises.*

Father, I thank You that Your work will not return to You void. Your Word will accomplish what You have declared."

Prayer of Forgiveness

"If we confess our sins, He is faithful and righteous to forgive us our sins, and to cleanse us from all unrighteousness." (1 John 1:9)

"Father, I thank You for Your unconditional love. Today Father, I ask You to forgive me for my sins against You, and others. Father, I ask You to bring to my memory and understanding all those that I have sinned against; so that wherever and however possible, I may ask their forgiveness.

Father, forgive me for not always obeying your Word. Father, forgive me for not praying as I should. Please, Father, forgive me for anger, un-forgiveness, pride, selfishness, arrogance, evil speaking, evil thoughts, lying, procrastination, and fear of man.

Father, forgive me for being upset regarding times that You did not answer my prayers in the manner or time frame that I expected answers.

Father, forgive me for anything and everything that I have done to hurt, mistreat, disrespect, or discourage any one.

Father, Your Word teaches us, that if we, 'have ought,' against anyone, we need to forgive. So today, I choose to forgive those who have hurt me; and I choose to forgive myself. I choose to embrace Your Word that, You will forgive my sins, cast them into the Sea of Forgetfulness and You will remember them no more. Thank You for Your forgiveness. Thank You Jesus for Your promises are, Yes and Amen!"

Prayer of Renunciation

"Therefore submit to God. Resist the devil and he will flee from you." (James 4:7 New King James Version)

"Father, I renounce every evil force of darkness that is attacking my life. I command it to go in Jesus name. According to Your Word, if I resist the devil, he will flee. So Lord, I renounce his attacks on my life."

Prayer of Peace

"Thou wilt keep him in perfect peace, whose mind is stayed on Thee; because he trusteth in Thee." (Isaiah 26:3)

"Depart from evil, and do good; Seek peace, and pursue it." (Psalm 34:14)

"And the peace of God, which passeth all understanding, shall guard your hearts and your thoughts in Christ Jesus." (Philippians 4:7)

"Father, Your Word teaches us to, seek peace and pursue it. We must run after our peace. Father, I thank You that when we are being distracted, distressed, disrespected, falsely accused, and discouraged, we can refuse the attack of the enemy by calling on the Name of Jesus and praising You. Father, thank You for enabling us to reject the problem, refuse the negative and embrace Your solution.

Father, Your Word says, My peace I give you; My peace I leave with you; not as the world gives. Father, I thank You, that I can go to sleep in peace, and I can wake up in the morning; in peace. Father I thank You for Your peace, which surpasses my understanding. Father, thank You for love, peace and joy in the Holy Ghost, Hallelujah!"

Prayer for Healing

"Bless Jehovah, O my soul, And forget not all his benefits: Who forgiveth all thine iniquities; Who healeth all thy diseases..." (Psalm 103:2-4)

"And when even was come, they brought unto Him many possessed with demons: and He cast out the spirits with a word, and healed all that were sick..." (Matthew 8:16-17)

"Heal the sick, raise the dead, cleanse the lepers, cast out demons: freely ye received, freely give." (Matthew 10:8)

"Jesus, I love You; I reverence You; I adore You; I delight in You.

Jesus, I thank You for taking my infirmities. Thank You for carrying my sorrows. I thank You that You were pierced for my transgressions; You were crushed for my iniquities; the punishment that brought me peace was upon You, and by Your stripes we are healed.

Jesus, manifest Your healing anointing in my life today. Father, I believe and I receive Your healing for me now. I receive spiritual healing, physical healing, mental healing, emotional healing, and financial healing.

Father, I thank You that healing is the children's bread. So today, Lord, I partake of my portion of bread daily.

Father, Your Word declares that Your desire is that we prosper and be in good health even as our souls prosper.

Father, I thank You for healing my mind, soul, body and my whole being in Jesus name."

CHAPTER 8

SUCCESS STORIES THROUGH PRAYER

SET FREE FROM DRUGS

My first husband gave our daughter, Pamela, marijuana at age twelve. Over twenty years she battled a drug addiction. Eight of those years, Pamela used cocaine. For three of those years, she was a major drug dealer. She said selling the drugs was more addictive than using them because of the big bucks.

God delivered Pam in 1988. In 1999 she began preaching the gospel of Jesus Christ. She is an intercessor, worshipper, and Bible teacher. When God delivered her, she said that she would be more tenacious for God than she was for drugs.

I was very aware of the call on Pam's life because at age seven she was playing preaching and singing. She would say to her friends, let's have sanctified church. I prayed, cried, declared and decreed life over her continually. Praise God for victory over that stronghold of drug addiction. Parents, may I encourage you, please don't stop praying for your children, regardless of what the situations look like, God is able to deliver them.

TRAVEL IN THE BEST SEATS

Since May 1998 I have been blessed to travel monthly. I routinely ask my Heavenly Father for a front window seat on each plane. In these thirteen years of travel, possibly as few as five times, I have been unable to receive the seat that I requested, even when traveling standby. Glory to Jesus! God is faithful. We must listen to Him, then pray, and then obey! The way we minister to God is by worshipping, praising and communing with Him in prayer.

"Draw near to God and He will draw near to you." (James 4:8)

GOD MOVED THE MILITARY

In 1977, my son and daughter-in-law were stationed in Japan, through the military. My son was being transferred back to the United States. His wife had one more year to her term in Japan, although she wanted to return home with him. I prayed that God would grant their request. They accepted Jesus and believed that He would answer their prayer. In faith, she came home with him before being released. Oops, she was AWOL!

The three of us went to Washington, D.C. to request a meeting with an officer. Six hours later after going from one office to another, we arrived at the Pentagon, trying to locate the admiral to speak with us.

A military police officer stepped in front of us and stopped me from entering the admiral's office, but the admiral heard me cry out. He came to the door and invited us into his office. I asked him, "Please Sir, will you allow my daughter to be transferred back to the United States with her husband?" The admiral sent us to a commanding officer.

The commanding officer said, "If I grant your request, every lady in the armed services will expect me to grant her request. Besides we only have one hour left before closing time." The three of us were crying and praying.

The commanding officer said, "I don't know why I'm doing this," as he called Japan and ordered that my daughter-in-law's belongings be sent to the United States. She had already packed everything prior to leaving Japan.

The government shipped all of her belongings to her in the United States and gave her a two week furlough with pay. When he finalized her orders, he repeatedly said, "I don't know why I'm doing this." I said to the commanding officer, "May I tell you why you are granting this request?" He said, "Yes." I said, "I prayed that God would touch someone's heart and allow my daughter to remain in the United States. Sir, it is Jesus that answered that prayer and I thank you."

I thank God that my daughter-in-law never returned to Japan. Several years later, she retired from the military after a twenty-year service record with an honorable discharge. Praise the Lord!

STATE TROOPER RECONCILED

In June 2010, a Pennsylvania State Trooper at the Greater Pittsburgh International Airport stopped to talk to me. I asked, "May I Pray With You?" His response was, "Yes." Several days after that prayer, he wrote me a note expressing how that prayer changed the course of his life and renewed his faith. He had been ready to give up hope in Jesus Christ. His hope has been restored. Glory to God!

GOD FIXED MY CAR

I owned a Toyota Camry. Someone hit my vehicle from the rear and left a huge dent in the bumper. I was not injured - praise God! But the damage to the car was estimated at $1,100 dollars to repair. I prayed that the Lord would 'heal my car.' A week later I went to the repairman. He examined my car and the damage was gone. Jesus fixed my car! Hallelujah!

JESUS CALMED MY DOCTOR

July 2011, I went to the hospital for an outpatient procedure. There was mass confusion in that procedure room. I asked the nurses, "May I Pray With You?" They responded, "Yes." After the prayer, the senior nurse came to me and said, "Thank you. I am an Orthodox Jew, but I desperately needed that prayer."

The doctor came into the room upset that a nurse did not have his patients ready. The doctor took my hand and asked, "How are you?" I grabbed his hand and said, "I'm fine." Continuing to hold his hand I began to pray.

"Father, in the name of Jesus, will you give this doctor Your peace. I thank You for the doctor. Thank You for his expertise. Thank You for his abilities. Thank You for these nurses. Thank You for the utensils being sterile and the anesthesiologist being alert. Father, I declare and decree peace in this room because I don't want this doctor working on me while he's upset, so I call forth Your peace in his heart now, in Jesus' name."

The doctor began to laugh and a calm, peaceful atmosphere entered the room. My procedure went well and I was fine. The doctor thanked me and I thanked Jesus for answered prayer.

NEW JOBS RECEIVED

Several years ago I prayed for a lady to receive a new job. We prayed that God would give her the position, the salary, the days off and the hours, that she desired. God granted her desires and answered that prayer. Hallelujah!

Another young lady finished college in 2010. I prayed the same prayer for her a job. God granted her desire and answered that prayer. Praise the Lord.

MISSING CHILD FOUND

I asked an employee of a restaurant in Missouri, *"May I Pray With You?"* The worker replied, "Yes," as she began to weep. The woman disclosed that her 16 year old daughter had been missing for several days. I prayed for the mother and for her daughter, asking that God would send the child home unharmed. The mother called me the next day stating that God answered that prayer and sent her daughter home unharmed!

OTHER TESTIMONIES

Since I travel monthly, many airport personnel across the USA get excited when they see me approaching saying, "Here comes 'The Lady that Prays.'" Often they will quickly service their current passenger to talk with me as they know that I will ask, *"May I Pray With You?"* Through the years, many call me by name and make known their prayer needs while they service me. I know it's not about me; it's all about JESUS!

Since May 2011, I frequently have been asked to travel to the Pennsylvania State Capitol, to pray with an international group of intercessors who focus on local and national issues. Routinely as part of these prayer times, I have had the blessing and opportunity to pray for Pastors, Attorneys, Judges, Senators, Governors and Lieutenant Governors, all serving constituents of Pennsylvania.

I have stood on the steps of the Capitol Rotunda in Harrisburg, Pennsylvania praying for the governor of Pennsylvania, his cabinet and the condition of our nation along with local pastors, elders and government officials. Routinely, many government officials request prayer for the state of our nation.

Several years ago, God healed me from the trauma, pain, and memories of sexual and verbal abuse inflicted on me by my step-father. On a recent trip to my birth state, as I sat in the driveway to the house where that horrific abuse took place, I was able to rejoice as I realized God's healing in my life and spirit. God is Faithful!

May 2011, I went to pray for a minister who was in an intensive care unit at a local hospital. A lady visiting with another family overheard me praying and requested that I pray for her son, who had been diagnosed with terminal cancer.

After praying for the young man, I asked if he desired to accept Jesus as his Savior. As he accepted Jesus as his Savior, he began screaming, "Thank You Jesus for saving me." The nurses, his mother, and his sister all received prayer that night. We were all crying. Two days later, his mother told me that his last words were, "Thank You Jesus for saving me." She said, "I know I will see him again. He's with Jesus."

Occasionally, people will decline prayer when asked, or respond, "No, I'm okay," or "I'm not very religious." I say, "Okay!" But as I leave them, I quietly pray for them anyway. I do this because I am not praying to them. I am praying to Jesus. We all need prayer, whether we know it, believe it or want it. Also when I recall their faces, I pray for them continually.

Prayer does not cause faith to work. Faith causes prayer to work.

FAITH CAUSES PRAYER TO WORK
MAY I PRAY WITH YOU?
Effective Prayer Without Ceasing

CHAPTER 9

UNEXPECTED OR UNDESIRED ANSWERS

We all sometimes feel that we've missed God's direction, instruction, or design for our lives. Here are a few of mine.

OBEDIENCE IS KEY!

Years ago, a pastor was celebrating his church anniversary. I was employed at his business and I had great respect for his wife. I was unable to attend the church anniversary celebration, because I had to work that night. (I actually had no desire to celebrate with them at their church because of that pastor's loose behavior.)

The Lord told me to send a $2.00 offering for the church anniversary. I was refusing to send the $2.00 because the person collecting the offering would say, "Sister Lucious sent $2.00." My pride didn't want people to know that I had sent that small amount. The lady that delivered the offering for me allowed them at the church to scream out, "Sister Lucious $2.00."

God spoke to me and said, "I'm teaching you obedience. If I say $5.00 and you give $50.00, that person is going to be blessed, but you have disobeyed Me. If I say $5.00 or $2.00 and you give $50.00, you are being disobedient. I am teaching you obedience and delivering you from pride.

Praise the Lord, I learned that lesson! Thank You Jesus!

Some time ago, I often helped a particular senior citizen. She began to experience dementia and I was concerned about her choices, behavior and safety. Her brother was pleading with her to move to Alabama and live with him and his family. The elderly lady refused to move unless I cleaned out her storage space. The Holy Spirit was leading me to decline. I was concerned about her living alone and wanted her to go with her brother and family.

I took three days to clean out her storage space of over 40 years worth of collected clothing and odds and ends. These things appeared to be junk to me; but they were her prized possessions. As a result of doing what I thought to be the "right thing," I developed an acute sinus infection which lasted for two years. I repented for over-riding the prompting of the Holy Spirit and disobeying God. God forgave me and healed me. Praise the Lord. Amen.

PAINFUL ANSWERS

My daughter, Elsia Marie Lucious Franklin called me in March of 2000 and said, "Mom sit down. I have been diagnosed with breast cancer." I was devastated. I prayed for her immediately and continued to pray. Elsia's condition seemed to grow worse as I fervently prayed for her. As the condition worsened, we declared Scripture in prayer, fasted, cancelled curses, cried and continued seeking the Lord. Through it all, we believed that God would heal her.

However, in 2003 Elsia was informed that the cancer had reached her brain giving her 3 or 4 months to live. I refused that diagnosis! I never ceased from praying, declaring, and decreeing Elsia's healing.

Elsia lived in Kansas with her husband and three children. Although she was in a hospital bed, she was able to remain in her home. Wanting to spend as much time with Elsia as I could, I slept on a couch directly across from her. Since I was in such close proximity to Elsia, I could sit facing her at eye-level. About every hour, Elsia would look me in the eyes, smile at me, and then turn her head. One morning around 5 a.m., Elsia looked me in the eyes, smiled, turned her head and went to sleep. The Lord revealed to me that Elsia was trying to slip away. I cried and asked God to help "me!"

Later that morning, my daughter, Kathi called having no knowledge of the early morning thoughts facing me or Elsia. However, Kathi asked Elsia, "Are you ready to go home with Jesus?" Elsia answered, "Yes." Kathi asked, "Are you ready to go home now?" Again, Elsia said, "Yes." Kathi asked, "Will you tell Mom or do you want me to tell her?" Elsia answered, "I don't care." Elsia called for her children and husband and encouraged them. Elsia told me, "Thanks Mom for everything, I love you."

Early the next morning, Elsia's husband, Bernard, the nurse, and I held hands and prayed with Elsia. While we held hands and prayed, we watched Elsia quietly slip away. I was deeply hurt and disappointed. I prayed, "God, Your promises are true and You said by Your stripes, she (Elsia) was healed. Father, help me to understand." As clearly as one hears a bell, I heard in my spirit, "I promised not to allow any more to come to you than you could bear. I alone know how much you can bear. Praise Me. She (Elsia) *is* healed and doing her *Victory Dance.*"

I learned *again* – that often God's answers to our prayers are the opposite of what we desire or expect. However, Hebrews 11:6 (New Amplified Version) says, "Without faith it is impossible to please Him for he who comes to God must believe that He is a rewarder of those who seek Him." Therefore, I trust that everything that He does in my life is for my good and for His glory. Amen!

"Father, I know that Your call upon my life includes being a servant, obeying Your command and always growing as an intercessor and a worshipper. Father, help me to do all of these things according to Your will. Please show me when I'm failing to do them. I know I've been called out of darkness into Your marvelous light to proclaim Your praises. All praise be to You, Oh Lord of heaven and earth, forever. Amen."

CONCLUSION

Beloved, after all the pages of terms, definitions, suggestions and recommendations on prayer; after all of the scriptural references, after all of the conditions are met and every detail is carefully lined up, the main desired result is that you will embrace, acknowledge, engage, respond to and obey the command in 1 Thessalonians 5:17:

"Pray without ceasing!"

God honors prayer! And God answers prayer!

An elaborate prayer of proper and distinguished words is impressive, but a humble prayer, from a sincere heart is what will move the heart of God.

Inevitably in your lifetime, someone will need you to pray for them and you will need someone to pray for you.

Everybody needs prayer.

Prayer is God's way for us to communicate with Him so that you may be able to touch the heart of God for the hearts of His people. God wants you to pray for the people of our families, the people of our cities, the people of our nations, all over the planet in the name of Jesus. I pray that every person reading this book will be blessed, encouraged, and enlightened to pray without ceasing. When you give yourself to God in prayer, never be surprised if the Holy Spirit prompts you to say,

May I Pray With You?

MAY I PRAY WITH YOU?
Effective Prayer Without Ceasing

ABOUT THE AUTHOR

Mrs. Carrie L. Porter is an intercessor, prayer warrior, encourager, and counselor. She prays scripture and will ask anyone in any setting, *"May I Pray With You?"* Ninety-eight percent respond, "Yes."

Deaconess Carrie is known nationally and internationally for ministering to pastor's wives and for loving and caring for God's people. She is a servant leader, and staff member of "Women Without Walls Call to Unity," Pittsburgh Chapter. She regularly prays at the Pennsylvania State Capitol, Harrisburg, Pennsylvania, with and for state senators, judges, lawyers, pastors, leaders and government officials.

She is a faithful member of Covenant Church of Pittsburgh (Pennsylvania) since 1971 under the leadership of Bishop Joseph and Pastor Barbara Garlington. She is affectionately known as Mom Porter.

Known to her family as Gram, Grammy and Grand, Mrs. Porter has many grand and great grandchildren, and a host of friend-children, adult children, and toddlers, who call her Mom, Mom Porter, and Grandma.

CITED REFERENCES

1 Prayers. Lexington, Kentucky: Christian Word Ministries.

2 Larson, Bob. *Larson's Book of Cults.* Wheaton, Illinois: Tyndale House Publishers, Inc., 1982, 19.

CPSIA information can be obtained at www.ICGtesting.com
Printed in the USA
BVOW040626080213

312702BV00001B/4/P